The be:

Came

ROGER PHILLIPS
& MARTYN RIX

Research by Alison Rix
Design Jill Bryan & Debby Curry

Acknowledgements

Most of the camellias photographed came from the following gardens and we are grateful to the owners and staff of these gardens for their help:
Marwood Hill Gardens, Devon; Caerhays Castle, Cornwall; Chiswick House, London; Exbury Gardens, Hampshire; The Royal Horticultural Society's Garden, Wisley; The Royal Botanic Gardens, Kew; Eccleston Square Gardens, London; Hillier Arboretum, Hampshire; Mount Edgcumbe, Cornwall; Trewithen, Cornwall; The Valley Gardens, Windsor Great Park; Coleton Fishacre, Devon; Arlington Court, Devon; Trehane Camellias, Dorset; Paradise Plants, Sydney; The US National Arboretum, Washington DC; Nuccio's Camellia Nurseries, Altadena, California; Descanso Gardens, California and Berkeley Botanical Garden, California.

Among others who have helped in one way or another we would like to thank:
Marilyn Inglis and Anne Thatcher.

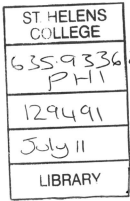

First published 1999 by Pan
an imprint of Macmillan Publishers Limited
25 Eccleston Place, London SW1W 9NF
and Basingstoke
Associated companies throughout the world
ISBN 0-330-37252-1
Copyright in the text and illustrations
© Roger Phillips and Martyn Rix
The right of the authors to be identified as the authors of this work has been asserted by them in accordance with the Copyright, Designs and Patents Act 1988.
9 8 7 6 5 4 3 2 1
A CIP catalogue record for this book is available from the British Library

Colour Reproduction by Aylesbury Studios Ltd.
Printed by Butler & Tanner Ltd. Frome, Somerset

Contents

Camellias

Camellias are very much part of our everyday lives; whenever we drink a cup of ordinary tea we are drinking an infusion of the tips of camellia shoots, grown in warm mountain climates in countries such as China, India, Sri Lanka or East Africa. Tea as a drink first arrived in England in the 17th century, but did not become popular till the mid-18th century. At that time it was imported from China, and the English – particularly the East India Company – tried to maintain a monopoly on the lucrative tea trade; the tax on tea was one of the main causes of the famous Boston Tea Party incident in 1773.

The tea clippers, those fast sailing ships, also brought back other goods from China: fine porcelain, silk cloth and Chinese garden plants, among them chrysanthemums, roses and the first ornamental camellias. The year 1739 is given for the introduction of the first *Camellia japonica*, and other varieties came over during the rest of that century; 1820 is the year of the arrival of *Camellia reticulata* 'Captain Rawes'.

Prior to their introduction to the West, camellias had been cultivated in China and Japan for thousands of years, first for the oil contained in their seeds and later for their ornamental qualities.

Camellia 'Akashigata' ('Lady Clare'). Flower semi-double: two or more rows of petals surround a mass of stamens, sometimes with a few petaloids

Camellia 'Maud Messel'. Flowers rose form, double: a regular double in which the stamens show in the open flower

The flower forms

The main flower shapes which we know today had already been selected in China and Japan by the time that camellias arrived

Single Higo flower: one whorl of broad petals surrounds a mass of perfectly developed stamens

Imbricate, formal double flower: the petals gradually become smaller towards the centre. In rare imbricated flower they seem to line up in rows

Anemone flower: the large outer petals are clearly distinct from the tight mass of inner ones

in Europe – single, semi-double, anemone-form, peony-form and formal double – still the main flower shapes known today. Examples of them are shown in these two pages. Another typically Japanese flower shape, the 'Higo', a wide open single with a mass of perfect stamens is also now found throughout the world.

Growing & siting plants

Most camellias are easy to grow provided they are given acid, leafy soil and sufficient water and warmth in summer. They grow best in warm, moist areas with summer rain or irrigation and a mild winter; northern Portugal, Madeira, Cornwall and the coast of California are ideal locations where fine collections of old camellias can be seen, but many of them are very tolerant of conditions which are not perfect, and in most gardens a suitable environment is easy to provide.

Acid soil Camellias are much more tolerant of slightly alkaline or neutral soils than are other ericaceous shrubs such as azaleas and rhododendrons. On neutral soils, most camellias will thrive with the addition of leaf-mould or peat to the soil. The soil may also be sprinkled with sulphur to make it more acid. On really chalky soils, it may be necessary to grow camellias in large tubs or in a specially built raised bed of acid soil. Provided that the water used for irrigation is not alkaline, this is a perfectly satisfactory arrangement, as the fleshy roots of camellias are tolerant of a little drought and form a compact mass.

Summer water Camellias grow naturally in areas which have most of their rainfall between June and September in the hot season and have relatively dry, cold winters. Therefore, in Mediterranean-type climates such as California, camellias need irrigation in summer, certainly until they are well established. Old shrubs planted in woodland and with a deep surface layer of leaves may survive the summer in the more coastal areas. Even in cities such as London, where camellias do very well, some summer water

may be needed in dry seasons. A mulch of leaf-mould and bark will help to retain any moisture that is around. Just a short period of drought between July and September may cause buds to drop off in winter, so it is important to water the plants thoroughly during dry spells, both by spraying the leaves and by watering directly onto the roots through the mulch.

Summer warmth Areas where camellias can survive the winter generally have warm enough summers for the formation of flower buds. In Scotland, however, and even in some areas of southern England and western North America, cool summers may be too cold for bud formation. If this is the suspected cause of non-flowering, the plants should be moved to a warmer position in the garden, even into full sun. *Camellia × williamsii* cultivars such as 'Donation' are said to flower better in cooler summer climates than most *C. japonica* cultivars.

Camellia japonica 'Her Majesty Queen Elizabeth II' Peony-form: the inner petals are smaller than the outer and form a confused mass

Winter cold   Winter hardiness is a complex subject, but some generalizations may be useful. Most camellias can survive 15°F (−10°C) overnight without damage. If the cold period lasts longer than a week, damage to leaves and buds will begin; more severe damage will follow longer cold spells and greater wind chill. More intense cold, even for a night, can kill the plants to ground level or back to old hard wood; 3°F (−16°C) is considered the temperature at which really serious damage occurs. Roots are even more tender, and potted plants should be kept frost-free in winter; a deep loose mulch of leaves or peat will protect the roots of established plants. Shelter from dry freezing wind and sun when the ground is frozen will help the plants survive. Even where the leaves and twigs are killed, old plants may sprout from below the following summer.

Camellia 'Salutation'

Planting

If the soil is sandy or well-drained already, it is sufficient to dig in ample leaf-mould or acid peat. If the soil is clay or poorly drained, make a raised planting area so that most of the roots are above the level which may become waterlogged, and fill the raised area with good compost. If the underlying soil is chalky or of high pH (more than 6.5), line the planting hole with a thick polythene sheet, perforated in a few places so that it can drain, but alkaline water cannot get back into the planting hole, and worms cannot mix the soil. This is the equivalent to planting in a large tub, so plants in a lined hole will need extra watering in dry weather. When planting out a potted camellia, be careful not to plant too deeply; the top couple of inches (5cm or so) of the rootball should be above soil level and covered only by mulch; this is the main zone of the feeding roots.

Problems

Camellias are generally trouble-free, but these are the commonest problems that may occur:

No buds   The summer temperature may be too cold for bud formation; in borderline areas move the shrubs to a warmer position in the garden, or put into tubs and keep in the greenhouse.

Bud drop   Buds which form properly but then drop off in autumn or winter have probably been affected by a spell of drought in summer. Keep the plants well watered from July to September.

Yellow leaves   Caused by the soil being too alkaline, by the plant being starved or by lack of water. In all cases this can be helped by exposing the surface roots, and top dressing with a loose layer of acid peat and a sequestrated iron plus fertilizer, as is sold for ericaceous plants. Watering the plants with cold tea and tea leaves will produce healthy leaf colour.

Black sooty mould deposit on leaves Caused by honeydew from aphids or scale insects becoming infected by moulds. The aphids may be on the camellia itself, in which case they should be removed, or they may be on an overhanging tree such as a lime or sycamore; in both cases spray the plant with soapy water and, if practical, sponge the leaves clean.

Old bushes of a single red at the Hillier Arboretum: the somewhat funnel-shaped flowers are typical of wild *Camellia japonica*

Camellia × williamsii 'Debbie'at Mount Edgcumbe: a tight peony-form to semi-double

Scale insects   A bad pest, forming either brown scales on the stems or white fluffy lines on the leaf backs. The plants should be sprayed with insecticide, ideally during early summer or in early autumn. At these seasons the young insects are active.

Aphids   Commonly called greenfly or blackfly, these may be green, black or brown, and generally infect young leaves; spray with a mild soap solution.

Vine weevils   Serious pests of camellias (and other plants with fleshy roots, particularly fuchsias and lilies) which are grown in pots, these may even kill young plants in the open ground. The adult black beetles, around ¼in (6mm) long, eat notches on the edges of young leaves, and these notches are a sign that vine weevils are present. It is the grubs that do the serious damage, by eating the roots and finally the bark of the plant at ground level; they are small, fat and white, and spend summer,

autumn and winter eating roots. Search for and destroy the beetles at night with a torch in early summer; in late summer drench the roots with an insecticide or a special nematode available from firms which specialize in biological control.

Propagation

Camellias are propagated in four main ways: by seed; by sports which produce new cultivars; by cuttings; and by grafting which produces new plants of the same cultivar.

Seed   Camellias are easy to raise from seed, provided the seed has not dried out. Plant seed that is as fresh as possible, and keep just moist and warm until the young leaves expand. One method recommended is to put the seeds in damp sphagnum or moss peat in a polythene bag in the airing cupboard until they are seen to be making roots. Pot up the seedlings, taking care to preserve the young shoots. Seedlings take from five years or more to flower.

Cuttings   Most varieties of camellia will root from cuttings, which are best taken in late July or early August in the northern hemisphere or February in the southern hemisphere. Use a new shoot, not too soft nor too woody, with three leaves. Remove the lowest, leaving the bud, but taking off a sliver of bark an inch (2.5cm) long opposite the bud. Put rooting hormone on the base and place the cutting in a mixture of ¾ moss peat or ground bark, ¼ acid sand. Put each cutting into a separate pot and cover with a polythene bag or bell cloche. Keep in as light

'Houye Diechi' or 'Butterfly Wings', an ancient Yunnan *Camellia reticulata*

Camellia petals at Trewithen, Cornwall

as possible a place, away from direct sunlight. Bottom heat will speed rooting, but is not necessary in summer.

Sports Many camellias produce different flowers on the same bush. These mutations, or sports as they are called, can be preserved by taking the shoot as a cutting and making a new plant which may represent a new variety or may be a sport which has occurred already. For example, 'Yours Truly' (*see this page and page 66*) occurred as a sport of 'Lady Vansittart', and may occur again.

Hybridizing your own camellias

Choose as female or seed parent a variety which has a good reputation for producing seeds; single flowers are usually good producers, as are many semi-doubles. In the text the first named parent is generally the seed parent and, like racehorses, some parents have a record of producing worthwhile progeny. To fertilize a flower, first remove all the stamens from an unopened flower without getting pollen onto the stigma. Also remove the petals and mark the treated flower; in a few days beads of sugar

may appear on the stigma of the emasculated flower, showing that the stigmas are receptive to pollen from the chosen pollen parent. Apply the pollen liberally, and label with the names of both parents. The fruit will begin to form in a few weeks, but not be ripe until the next autumn. Contamination with unwanted pollen by insects is unlikely if the petals have been removed, so it is not necessary to cover the treated flower. Successful fertilization is more likely in warm weather, or in a greenhouse, as the pollen tubes which travel from the stigma to the ovary grow best in moderate heat.

'Yours Truly', a sport of 'Lady Vansittart'

Camellia nitidissima at Nuccio's Nurseries

Camellia sinensis near Ya-an, in Sichuan

Camellia grijsii at Trehane's Nursery

Camellia Species

There are about 230 wild species of camellia, found from the eastern Himalayas and south China to Japan in the east and Malaysia in the south. Most of them form small trees and bushes with simple, evergreen, leathery leaves and grow in subtropical forest, particularly along streams. A range of species is cultivated, either for tea (*Camellia sinensis*) or for oil, which is extracted from the large seeds of several species, especially *C. oleifera*, a white-flowered species from China. Camellias belong to the family *Theaceae*, which includes deciduous trees such as *Stewartia* and the unique *Franklinia alatamaha*, now extinct in its native Georgia, but preserved in gardens.

PLANTING HELP   All camellias grow best in leafy, slightly acid soil and in slight shade, except in very dull climates. Shelter from drying wind will also help those on the borders of hardiness. They should have ample water in summer, but may be drier in winter. A mulch of leaf-mould or bark will help retain water in summer, and watering with old tea will act as fertilizer to plants in pots or in areas with chalky water. Hardiness varies according to the origin of the species.

Camellia crapnelliana   A small tree around 24ft (7m) tall with beautiful smooth, red-brown bark, shiny green leaves and brown, tangerine-sized fruit. Native to SW China, on hills near Hong Kong. Flowers white, to 4in (10cm) across, with 6–8 narrow petals, in late autumn. Hardy to 32°F (0°C), US zone 10.

Camellia cuspidata   A graceful shrub 10ft (3m) tall with acuminate leaves and masses of small white flowers in early spring. Native to central China, in Hubei and Sichuan, growing in open woods. Leaves to 2½in (6cm) long, coppery when young. One of the hardiest species, parent of the small-flowered hybrids 'Cornish Snow' and 'Cornish Spring'. Hardy to 20°F (–6°C), US zones 9–10.

Camellia grijsii   A small shrub 10ft (3m) tall with ovate leaves and white flowers in winter and early spring, wild in central China, in Hubei. Leaves 1½–3in (4–8cm) long, with numerous fine teeth. Flowers 1½–2½in (4–6cm) across, with obovate petals, indented at the tip. Similar to *C. sasanqua*, but flowering mainly in spring. Hardy to 20°F (–6°C), US zones 9–10.

Camellia nitidissima (syn. *C. chrysantha*) An upright shrub or small tree with large, rather thin, pale green leaves to 6½in (17cm) long, with conspicuous veins and bright yellow flowers to 2in (5cm) across in winter and spring; it grows wild in N Vietnam and SW China. Not easy to grow well in the greenhouse, making new growth in both spring and autumn, needing a dry winter and a wet and humid summer. Hardy to 32°F (0°C), US zone 10.

Tea *Camellia sinensis* A shrub or small tree 20ft (6m), or in Assam tea (var. *assamica*) to 50ft (15m) or more, with rather thin, dark green leaves and small white flowers 1½in (4cm) across. When grown for tea, the plants are kept as low hedges so that young shoots with one or two leaves can be picked for drying. Hardy to 32°F (0°C), US zone 10.

Camellia crapnelliana

Camellia crapnelliana in the Shing Mun Arboretum

Camellia cuspidata at Caerhays Castle, Cornwall

Camellia 'Uraku-tsubake'

Camellia yunnanensis at Nuccio's Nurseries

Camellia yunnanensis A shrub or small tree that grows to 20ft (6m) with smooth, finely toothed leaves and white flowers around 1½in (4cm) across, with conspicuous yellow stamens in late summer and autumn. This species is wild in Yunnan and S Sichuan, at up to 7000ft (2000m) in the Dali area, so should be hardy to 20°F (−6°C), US zones 9–10.

Camellia saluenensis A shrub that grows to 17ft (5m) with oval, finely toothed leaves and cup-shaped flowers about 2½in (6cm) across in spring, found wild in the mountains of western China, flowering in late winter and spring. The flowers are usually pink, but may be white or red. This species was introduced to Europe by the plant hunter George Forrest in around 1917 and is important as a parent of the very free-flowering × *williamsii* hybrids, such as the popular 'Donation'. Hardy to 10°F (−12°C), US zones 8–10 or possibly in the warmer parts of zone 7.

***Camellia saluenensis* 'Exbury Trumpet'** A very good form of *C. saluenensis* with broad spreading petals and typical small leaves. Early-flowering with flowers of good substance to withstand the weather.

Camellia 'Shôwa-wabisuke' (syn. 'Apple Blossom' and 'Little Princess') An ancient Chinese or Japanese variety, recognized by its narrow leaves and small, single flowers. The Wabisuke group of small-flowered camellias were a speciality of the Kyoto district, though the original of the group was imported from China, and was possibly a hybrid between *C. japonica* and

C. sinensis. About 120 varieties of Wabisuke are known today. Hardy to 10°F (−12°C), US zones 8–10. 'Apple Blossom' is sometimes listed under *C. saluenensis* but the leaves are typical of *C. japonica*.

Camellia 'Uraku-tsubake' (syn. 'Tarôkaja') An old Chinese or Japanese Wabisuke cultivar, first recorded in 1739. Flowers on the large side for Wabisuke, with broad overlapping petals and degenerate stamens. This variety is now found both in Japan and in China.

Camellia fraterna A graceful weeping shrub, 17ft (5m) tall, with shiny oval leaves and small white scented flowers 1½in (4cm) across in spring, found wild in SE China. The twigs and young leaves are bristly hairy. Hardy to 32°F (0°C), US zone 10.

Camellia fraterna

Camellia saluenensis 'Exbury Trumpet'

Camellia saluenensis at Caerhays Castle, Cornwall

Camellia 'Shôwa-wabisuke'

Camellia fraterna at Marwood Hill, Devon

Camellia saluenensis

Camellia sasanqua 'Crimson King' at Coleton Fishacre, Devon

Camellia sasanqua 'Crimson King'

Camellia sasanqua 'Agnes O. Solomon'

Camellia sasanqua 'Paradise Hilda'

Camellia sasanqua

Camellia sasanqua and its varieties are valuable for flowering from September to December. In the past, the leaves were used to make a rather inferior tea, and oil from the seeds was used for lighting, lubrication, cooking and cosmetics. There are numerous cultivars, mostly with single or double pink or red flowers, raised in Japan and in California; some are scented. All are hardy to 10°F (−12°C), US zones 8–10.

PLANTING & PRUNING HELP   In order to grow and flower well, sasanqua camellias need more heat than varieties of *C. japonica* and *C. × williamsii*. In northern Europe and in cooler areas on the west coast of North America, they should be planted on warm south- or west-facing walls. In areas with hot summers, no such problems will arise. Sasanquas tend to make long shoots, and these can be shortened in spring or even in midsummer as well to keep the plants compact.

Camellia sasanqua   A shrub that grows to 20ft (6m) tall with oval glossy leaves. The pink or white flowers are 2–2¾in (5–7.5cm), with 6–8 petals. In the wild, white flowers are produced from October to December; it is found in Japan growing in openings in woods in Kyushu and the islands further south, and I have seen it in the primaeval *Cryptomeria* forests on the island of Yakushima.

Camellia sasanqua 'Agnes O. Solomon'
Raised by the Orton Plantation Nursery in 1953–4; a soft pink, semi-double to peony-form with wavy petals.

CAMELLIA SASANQUA

Camellia sasanqua red form

Camellia sasanqua in the Washington Arboretum

C. sasanqua 'Mine-no-yuki'

Camellia sasanqua 'Crimson King'
Camellia sasanqua **'Crimson King'**
A Japanese variety which forms a dense bush
around 7ft (2m) tall, with single or semi-double
red flowers 4¾in (12cm) across with 6–8 petals
and conspicuous stamens. Introduced to Europe
by Wada's nursery in 1937.

Camellia sasanqua 'Mine-no-yuki'
Camellia sasanqua **'Mine-no-yuki'**
(syn. 'White Dove') A bushy, pendulous shrub
around 7ft (2m) tall, producing small, semi-
double, fragrant creamy flowers, from mid-
autumn to early winter.

Camellia sasanqua 'Narumigata'
Camellia sasanqua **'Narumigata'**
An upright or spreading shrub to 15ft (4.5m) tall,
producing single white, fragrant flowers about
2½–3in (6–8cm) wide, slightly tinged with pink, in
late autumn and early winter.

Camellia sasanqua 'Paradise Hilda'
Camellia sasanqua **'Paradise Hilda'**
Flowers mid-pink, semi-double. The Paradise
series is a group of new, free-flowering cultivars
raised by Bob Cherry of Paradise Plants near
Sydney, New South Wales. Roger photographed
this new variety in Australia.

'Narumigata'

C. 'Winter's Rose' in the Washington Arboretum

'Hugh Evans'

C. 'Winter's Hope' in the Washington Arboretum

Camellia sasanqua 'Cotton Candy'
(syn. 'Heyman's Pink') An American variety,
introduced by Barrio's Nursery in around 1955.
Flowers large, semi-double, with ruffled petals.
Shrub dense and spreading.

Camellia sasanqua 'Chojiguruma'
An upright shrub to 8ft (2.5m). Flowers 2½–2¾in
(6–7cm) across, beginning in early autumn. An
anemone-flowered variety, known in Japan since
1789. The Japanese name means wheel of
anemone.

Camellia sasanqua 'Hugh Evans'
(syn. 'Hebe') A strong-growing shrub with
single, medium-sized pink flowers produced in
autumn. The weeping branches enable it to be
easily trained on a post or fence. Hardy to 10°F
(−12°C), US zones 8–10.

C. 'Winter's Fire' in the Washington Arboretum

Camellia 'Winter's Charm' A winter-
flowering sasanqua-like camellia raised by Dr W.L.
Ackerman in Ashton, Maryland, by crossing
Camellia sasanqua 'Taka-awase' with *C. oleifera*,
introduced in 1988. Flowers around 3in (8cm)
across, with 14 petals and 14 petaloids, and
golden-yellow anthers. Shrub rather upright.
Hardy to −10°F (−23°C), US zones 5–10. Heat-
tolerant in summer.

C. 'Winter's Charm' in the Washington Arboretum

Camellia sasanqua 'Cotton Candy'

Camellia sasanqua 'Chojiguruma'

Camellia sasanqua 'Paradise Vanessa'

Camellia **'Paradise Vanessa'** Raised by Bob Cherry in his Paradise Nursery in Australia. Vigorous, rather upright growth, with large semi-double white flowers with pink buds which show as pink touches on the edges of the open petals, the flowers are very large for a Sasanqua up to 5in (12cm) across. Hardy to 10°F (−12°C), US zones 8–10.. Heat-tolerant in summer.

Camellia **'Winter's Rose'**
A sasanqua-like camellia raised by Dr W.L. Ackerman in Ashton, Maryland, by crossing *Camellia oleifera* with *C. hiemalis*. A shrub with miniature, pink double flowers 2in (5cm) across, with around 28 petals, produced in winter. Introduced in 1985, and remarkably hardy, reputedly to −10°F (−23°C), US zones 6–10.

Camellia **'Winter's Fire'** A winter-flowering sasanqua-like camellia raised by Dr W.L. Ackerman in Ashton, Maryland. A single flower with about 8 petals of a good deep pink, with yellow stamens, produced in winter. Remarkably hardy reputedly to −10°F (−23°C), US zones 6–10.

Camellia **'Winter's Hope'** A sasanqua-like camellia raised by Dr W.L. Ackerman in Ashton, Maryland, by crossing *Camellia oleifera* with the hybrid 'Frost Princess'. A spreading shrub with leaves around 2½in (6cm) long; flowers white, semi-double, around 3½in (9cm) across, with around 12 petals and yellow anthers, produced in winter. Introduced in 1985. Remarkably hardy, reputedly to −10°F (−23°C), US zones 6–10.

A single *Camellia japonica* in the Lingering Garden, Suzhow

Camellia japonica

More than half the cultivated camellia varieties grown today belong to the species *Camellia japonica*. It has been cultivated for ornament in China and Japan since at least the 12th century, but before that was grown as a source of oil from its seeds. The first plants reached England in 1702. It is now grown in all parts of the world with a suitable climate. Some of the finest new cultivars have been raised in California, New Zealand and Australia. *Camellia japonica* is long-lived, eventually forming small trees to 40ft (12m) or more tall.

PLANTING & PRUNING HELP   Plant camellias in autumn or late spring, either in a well-drained acid or neutral soil, using plenty of humus, preferably leaf-mould, but otherwise peat, or in special ericaceous compost. It is most important that the soil is well-drained, as water-logging of the plants is fatal. They require cool winters, and many will tolerate mild frosts, but they need warmth and sunlight in late summer to form flower buds. Camellias benefit when sheltered from cold winds and the early morning sun, and are happiest in areas of light shade under mature trees, as buds and flowers may be damaged by icy winds and late frosts. Unless otherwise stated, varieties of *C. japonica* can withstand 10°F

(−12°C) without serious damage, and are therefore suitable for most of US zone 8. Being heat-tolerant, they will grow in zone 11 but will need shade and water in areas with hot, dry summers. Camellias can be grown successfully in a greenhouse, either in the ground or in pots. Once established, all camellias benefit from the addition of some fertilizer, but be careful not to over-fertilize. Water well, regularly but infrequently in summer, sparingly in winter.

Little pruning is needed, although long shoots on young plants can be shortened to encourage branching; flowering time is the ideal time to prune, and any flowers that are cut off can be brought indoors and put in a vase. Propagate

Camellia japonica in Cornwall

CAMELLIA JAPONICA

Camellia japonica 'Aitonia' at Chiswick House

camellias by means of semi-ripe cuttings in late summer or by leaf-bud cuttings in spring. Scale insects, which produce an unsightly sooty mould on the leaves, may attack the young shoots and leaves, but camellias are not generally affected by pests. Spray with insecticide against young scale in the spring if there are signs of infestation.

Camellia japonica   Wild *Camellia japonica* is found in Japan on the islands of Honshu, Shikoku and Kyushu, growing in woods and along streams in the forest. The flowers are usually red, single and produced from February to June according to altitude. In the lowland variety, the flowers are rather cup-shaped, but the upland variety, the so-called Snow Camellia, subsp. *rusticana*, has flatter, more open flowers. On Yakusima is found the Apple Camellia, with fruit the size of small apples. Large areas of wild-looking red camellias are grown in Cornish gardens, where they were originally planted for selling as cut foliage for flower arranging; one variety with small red flowers has exceptionally glossy leaves. Another has sweetly scented flowers, a feature which is especially noticeable on a warm winter's day.

Camellia japonica 'Aitonia'   An old variety, raised by Alfred Chandler at Vauxhall, near London in 1819. The 6 petals have distinct veins, and the stamens are conspicuous. This variety is

reported to set seed well. Shown here are old plants, still growing in the Camellia House at Chiswick House.

Camellia japonica 'Bright Buoy'   Flowers about 2¾in (7cm) wide with overlapping petals, surrounding red filaments and golden stamens. Raised by Les Jury in New Zealand around 1968. Hardy to 20°F (–6°C), US zones 9–10, more tender than most varieties of *C. japonica*.

'Bright Buoy'

CAMELLIA JAPONICA

Camellia japonica 'Jupiter'

Camellia japonica 'California'

C. japonica 'Eiraku' at Nuccio's Nurseries

Camellia japonica 'Alexander Hunter'

Camellia japonica 'Alexander Hunter'
(sometimes abbreviated to 'Alex Hunter')
A moderately vigorous shrub of upright habit,
with good single red flowers which have
particularly attractive golden stamens. Raised in
Sydney, Australia by Alexander Hunter in 1884
and named after him by G.C. Linton.

Camellia japonica 'California' (syns. 'Durfee
Road', 'Durfee Road Pink')   A compact but
vigorous shrub to 12ft (3.5m) tall, with large, semi-

Camellia japonica 'California' at the Huntington Botanical Gardens, San Marino, California

double rose-red flowers to about (4in) 10cm across. The original plant, bought in Los Angeles from a sailor on a Japanese steamer, was grown in Durfee Road, Pico, California, hence the synonyms. Blooms in spring.

Camellia japonica **'Eiraku'** (syn. 'Kuro-wabisuke') An upright but slow-growing shrub with beautifully simple, single, dark red flowers. Raised in Ikeda City, Osaka Prefecture, Japan by Katayama in 1957.

Camellia japonica **'Jupiter'** (syn. 'Juno') A vigorous, free-flowering shrub of upright habit, eventually reaching up to about 15ft (4.5m). The single, deep reddish-pink flowers with overlapping petals are quite large, to about 3½in (9cm) across, and are produced in mid-spring. Particularly good, glossy, dark green foliage. Introduced into cultivation in about 1900 by William Paul of Cheshunt, England.

Camellia japonica **'Kimberly'** (syn. 'Crimson Cup') A vigorous shrub with an upright habit, with small, single, saucer-shaped, deep red flowers to about 2¾in (7cm) in diameter, with contrasting yellow staminodes. Introduced into cultivation (possibly from Japan) by Messrs Sander of Bruges, Belgium in about 1900.

'Kimberly'

CAMELLIA JAPONICA

C. japonica 'Dr Burnside' in Eccleston Square

Camellia japonica **'Adolphe Audusson'**
(numerous syns. including 'Audrey Hopfer')
A deservedly well-known vigorous, upright shrub
to 20ft (6m) tall and producing an abundance of
large, semi-double, pinkish-red flowers to about
4in (10cm) across, with a good boss of yellow
stamens in the centre. One of the hardiest
varieties. Raised in France by M. Audusson of
Angers in 1877.

Camellia japonica **'Bob Hope'**   An upright,
rather slow-growing medium-sized shrub with
dense dark green foliage, which eventually reaches
about 10ft (3m). The large dark red, semi-double
flowers are about 4in (10cm) wide and appear
from mid- to late spring. Raised by Nuccio's
Nurseries of Altadena, California in the 1960s.

Camellia japonica **'Dr Burnside'**   An upright
shrub with dark red flowers about 6in (15cm)
across, of loose semi-double or peony form. A
chance seedling which first bloomed in the garden
of Dr A.F. Burnside in 1959 in Columbia, South
Carolina, USA. Flowers in mid-spring. 'Dr
Burnside Variegated' (*not illustrated here*) is a sport
and has dark red flowers blotched with white.

Camellia japonica **'Dr King'**   A bushy, upright
shrub whose leaf margins are particularly serrated.
The large, semi-double flowers are light red. This
originated in Australia and has been in cultivation
since the 1940s. Flowers in mid-spring.

Camellia japonica **'Senator Duncan U.
Fletcher'**   A cultivar with an upright habit but
rather slow-growing. The foliage is often rather
twisted. Flowers peony-form, dark red, borne
from mid- to late spring. Introduced in the USA
by Gerbings in 1941.

Camellia japonica 'Dr King'

Camellia japonica 'Senator Duncan U. Fletcher'

'Bob Hope'

Camellia japonica 'Adolphe Audusson' at Exbury Gardens, Hampshire

'Arajishi'

Camellia japonica 'Mathotiana Supreme'

Camellia japonica 'Althaeiflora'

Camellia japonica 'Althaeiflora'
(syns. 'Childsii', 'Rosette', 'Thunbergia')
A vigorous shrub with an upright habit which
becomes more branched and spreading when
older. The carmine flowers are peony-form, to
about 4¼in (11cm) across with up to 18 outer
petals and numerous darker inner ones. A seedling
of 'Anemoniflora' which was raised at the Vauxhall
Nursery in London in 1819.

Camellia japonica 'Arajishi' (numerous syns.
including 'Arejishi')   A bushy shrub with
particularly long, narrow, rather light green leaves.
The flowers are small, to about 3in (8cm) across,
dark red, sometimes splashed with white and
usually peony-form. An old Japanese cultivar,
known since 1877 in Yokohama, this was
introduced into Europe in 1891. Flowers in
early spring.

Camellia japonica 'Mathotiana Supreme'
(syn. 'Mima-Mae')   In spite of its name, this is a
sport of *C. japonica* 'Julia Drayton', rather than of
C. 'Mathotiana'. Like its parent this is a vigorous
upright grower, with very large, dark red semi-
double flowers to about 4½in (12cm) across. The
stamens appear amongst the central boss of
irregularly shaped petals. Raised in the USA by
Flowerwood Nurseries, Alabama.

Camellia japonica 'Red Moon'   A vigorous
but compact variety, this has large, deep red semi-
double flowers, with a cluster of small petals in the
centre. Raised in Australia by E.G. Waterhouse.
There is also a form, known as 'Red Moon
Variegated' with white blotches on the petals (*not
shown here*).

Ancient *Camellia japonica* in a garden in China

Camellia japonica 'Red Moon' at Mount Edgcumbe

Camellia japonica 'Brilliant' at the Huntington Botanical Gardens, San Marino, California

C. japonica 'Tinsie' at Nuccio's Nursery

Camellia japonica 'Bob's Tinsie' A compact but upright-growing plant, with small leaves and very striking small – not more than 2½in (6cm) across – bright red anemone-form flowers in mid-spring. The central boss of petaloids looks almost chrysanthemum-like, being very regularly arranged, with each incurved petal having a small flash of pale pink on the upper edge. Does well in sun. Raised by Nuccio's Nurseries, Altadena, California.

'Bob's Tinsie'

Camellia japonica 'Grand Slam'

CAMELLIA JAPONICA

Camellia japonica 'Bob's Tinsie' at Mount Edgcumbe

***Camellia japonica* 'Brilliant'** (syns. 'Blackwell's Special', 'Tutcheria', 'Paloma', 'Poorman's Purple Dawn') A bushy plant with an upright habit and fully double red flowers in mid-spring. Raised by Blackwell in the USA about 50 years ago.

***Camellia japonica* 'Grand Slam'** A vigorous, upright shrub with good glossy leaves and dark red flowers to 5in (13cm) across, more if grown under glass. The blooms are variable, some of them being anemone-form, and others semi-double. Originated as a seedling in Nuccio's Nurseries, California, it has long been very popular in the USA.

***Camellia japonica* 'Tinsie'** (syn. 'Bokuhan') A vigorous grower, making a rather wider bush than its offspring (*see above*), with small deep red anemone-form flowers, to 2in (5cm) across in mid-spring. Central bosses of white petaloids contrast nicely with the outer red petals. A very old variety, known since 1719 and possibly earlier, which originated in Kantô District, Japan, and was imported into the USA by the Star Nursery, California during the 1930s.

***Camellia japonica* 'Pensacola Red'** (syn. 'Pensacola') A vigorous, upright grower with large, dark red peony- to anemone-form flowers and red filaments in spring. Raised by Bowman, Florida, USA.

'Pensacola Red'

27

CAMELLIA JAPONICA

Camellia japonica 'Coquettii' in the Valley Gardens, Windsor Great Park

Camellia japonica 'Christmas Beauty'
(syn. 'Christmas') A vigorous upright shrub that
has glossy, dark green leaves with serrated edges
and large, red, semi-double flowers early in the
spring. The petals are attractively fluted. An
old variety raised by V. Howell of
Mississippi, USA. There is also a sport
'Christmas Beauty Variegated'
(*not illustrated*), whose red flowers are
blotched with white.

Camellia japonica 'Coquettii'
(syns. 'Alabama', 'Coquette', 'Glen 40',
'Incomparabilis Vera') A compact, slow-
growing but upright plant with attractive,
dark glossy green foliage and deep red,
formal double flowers to about 4in (10cm)
across. A seedling raised by M. Tourres
of Macheteau, France, this was first
described in 1839. 'Coquettina'
(*not illustrated here*) is a sport with
deeper red flowers and sometimes
white stripes.

**Camellia japonica 'Forest
Green'** A vigorous, upright-growing
but compact plant, this has long, dark
green leaves and medium-sized red, formal
double flowers in mid- to late spring. Raised by
Harvey Short of California, USA.

Camellia japonica 'Konronkoku' (syns. 'Black
Boy', 'Black Prince', 'Nigra'; also translated in
many different ways, e.g. 'Konron-Koku',
'Konronkuro', 'Konron Joura') A variety with
medium-sized, rose-form double to peony-form
dark red flowers, to about 4in (10cm) across.
Introduced to Britain from Japan by Col Sir James
Horlick in 1939.

'Christmas Beauty'

Old camellias along the drive at Quinta de Palheiro Ferreiro in Madeira

***Camellia japonica* 'Winter Cheer'**
A compact, bushy shrub with medium-sized, semi-double, rose-red flowers in spring. It occurred earlier this century as a seedling under a plant of 'Tricolor' in Treseder's Nursery, in New South Wales, Australia.

'Winter Cheer'

Camellia japonica 'Konronkoku'

Camellia japonica 'Forest Green'

29

***Camellia japonica* 'Kumasaka'**   This has large double pink flowers, sometimes streaked with red, varying in form from peony- to semi-double or rose-form. A very old variety, dating back to the 17th century and possibly earlier, this is another camellia which originates from the Kantô district of Japan.

***Camellia japonica* 'Niobé'** (syn. 'Le Niobé') A large-flowered variety with bright pink, rose-form double blooms to about 4in (10cm) across. Raised in Italy by Mariani.

***Camellia japonica* 'Rainy Sun'**   A good, tough, loosely upright shrub with glossy, dark green serrated leaves and medium-sized, semi-double pinkish-red flowers to about 3in (8cm) across. Its exact origins are uncertain, but it is thought to have come from Japan.

Camellia japonica 'Rainy Sun'

Camellia japonica 'Niobé' at Mount Edgcumbe

***Camellia japonica* 'Rubescens Major'**
A compact and densely bushy shrub, with good broad, glossy leaves and lovely rose-form flowers to about 4in (10cm) across. The petals are rose-red, with deeper red veining, and there is usually a central group of petals which open only at a very late stage. An old and reliable variety, raised in Nantes, France in the 1890s by Guichard Soeurs. 'Rubescens Major Variegated' is a sport *(not illustrated)*.

'Rubescens Major'

C. japonica 'Kumasaka' at Mount Edgcumbe

Camellia japonica 'Rubescens Major' in the conservatory at Arlington Court, Devon

CAMELLIA JAPONICA

Camellia japonica 'Sunset Glory'

Camellia japonica 'Casablanca'

Camellia japonica 'Elizabeth Weaver'

Camellia japonica 'Mrs Tingley'

Camellia japonica 'Pink Pagoda'

CAMELLIA JAPONICA

Camellia japonica **'Casablanca'** (several syns. including 'Bleichroeder Pink' in the USA) A very attractive, pale pink formal double, which produces medium-sized blooms in mid-spring. This arose as a sport of 'Otome-shibori' (also known as 'Huntington').

'Pink Pagoda'

Camellia japonica **'Elizabeth Weaver'** A medium-sized shrub, this bears large, to 4½in (12cm) across, very beautiful coral-pink formal double flowers in early spring. This cross between 'Elizabeth Boardman' and 'Clarise Carleton' was made by Dr W. Homeyer of Georgia, USA and bloomed for the first time in 1967.

Camellia japonica **'Mrs Anne Marie Hovey'** An upright grower, this extraordinary old cultivar is particularly notable for the variety of flower colours it can produce. The large, formal double flowers may be white, white with crimson markings, many shades of pink or carmine, or sometimes half white and half pink; our specimen is a rather understated pink with a few blotches of white. Raised by C.M. Hovey of Boston, Massachusetts, USA; details of this plant were first published in his *Catalogue of New Plants* for 1872. The Royal Horticultural Society obviously thought it merited attention as it was awarded a First Class Certificate in 1897.

Camellia japonica **'Mrs Tingley'** This variety has an upright, open habit of growth and formal double blooms early in the season. The flowers can measure up to 4in (10cm) across, with salmon-pink petals; in the centre is a group of darker pink, smaller petals which never completely open. Raised by J.H. Ward Hinkson of Pennsylvania, USA.

Camellia japonica **'Pink Pagoda'** A robust, compact, upright plant. The attractive formal double, rose-pink flowers measure up to about 4in (10cm) across and appear in mid-spring. The sport 'Pink Pagoda Variegated' (*not illustrated here*) has pink flowers blotched with white.

Camellia japonica **'Sunset Glory'** This shrub is distinguished by its large, deep pink blooms which have a central boss of petaloids, that may measure up to 5in (13cm) across. *Camellia japonica* 'Sunset Glory' was first raised by Harvey Short of California, USA.

Camellia japonica 'Mrs Anne Marie Hovey' at Mount Edgcumbe

Camellia japonica 'Tomorrow'

Camellia japonica 'Dewatairin'

Camellia japonica 'Preston Rose'

Camellia japonica 'Guest of Honor'

Camellia japonica 'Dewatairin' (numerous syns. including 'Daitairin') An early-flowering cultivar with large rose-pink anemone-form flowers, 4½in (12cm) across, with a mass of petaloids in the centre. Origin uncertain, but possibly a very old Japanese variety. There is a sport with white blotches on the flowers named 'Manzairaku' (*not illustrated*).

Camellia japonica 'Eugene Lizé' (numerous syns. including 'Annie McDonald', 'Archie McDonald', 'Lady Jane Grey') A slow-grower with a loose but upright habit and good, glossy, elliptic-shaped leaves. The peony-form flowers

Camellia japonica 'Eugene Lizé'

Pink japonicas at Caerhays Castle, Cornwall

usually appear early in the spring and are rose-pink blotched with white, and measure up to about 4in (10cm) across. Raised by Mathurin Lizé of Nantes in the 1880s and listed by Guichard Soeurs in their 1894 catalogue under the name 'Donkelaari Eugene Lizé'.

Camellia japonica **'Guest of Honor'**
A cultivar with large peony-form flowers, to 4½in (12cm) across; the petals are rose-pink veined with deeper pink. A seedling of 'Lotus', raised by Harvey F. Short of California, USA.

Camellia japonica **'Preston Rose'** A robust, upright plant with good, glossy, dark green leaves with serrated edges and attractive pink flowers. The flowers are about 3½in (9cm) across, double peony-form and have a mass of petaloids in the centre. Its parentage is unknown, but this camellia

is thought to have originated in France, where it is erroneously known as 'Duchesse de Rohan', as it was described in a French nursery catalogue in 1840.

Camellia japonica **'Tomorrow'** A quick-growing cultivar with a loose, slightly pendulous, habit. The large, deep pink flowers appear early in the season and can measure up to 6in (15cm) across. They are incomplete double in form, with many petaloids. Raised at Tick Tock Nursery, Georgia, USA, where it first bloomed in 1950. When given an Award of Merit by the Royal Horticultural Society in 1960 it was recommended 'for cultivation in cool greenhouse conditions' in Britain. It has given rise to an enormous number of sports, too numerous to list here, but they can usually be spotted as they have the word 'Tomorrow' as part of their name.

CAMELLIA JAPONICA

'Akashigata'

Camellia japonica 'Constance' A deep pink semi-double, surrounding a prominent boss of deep yellow stamens. Raised at Camellia Grove, New South Wales, Australia, in 1941.

Camellia japonica 'Guilio Nuccio'
A deservedly popular and award-winning camellia, which eventually makes an upright shrub to about 20ft (6m), flowering in mid-spring. The long leaves have serrated margins, and occasionally, forked tips (*see below*). Very large semi-double flowers, up to 6in (15cm) across, are pinkish-red with slightly recurved outer petals and inner petals surrounding a group of deep yellow stamens. A seedling of 'Mermaid' (sometimes known as the 'fishtail camellia', because of the forked tip of the leaf) this plant was raised in the USA in 1955. It has given rise to four sports, all with 'Guilio Nuccio' in the name. (*not illustrated here*).

Camellia japonica 'Her Majesty Queen Elizabeth II' A compact camellia, this has deep pink medium-sized flowers of semi-double to peony-form, with slightly waved petals. Flowers in mid-spring. Raised as a seedling by Rubel and named in USA in 1953.

Camellia japonica 'Akashigata' or **'Lady Clare'** (other syns. 'Empress', 'Nellie Bly') A vigorous, low-growing variety which makes a wide, spreading bush with horizontal or drooping branches. The leaves are large, broad and pointed with toothed edges. The large semi-double rose-

Camellia japonica 'HM Queen Elizabeth II'

Camellia japonica 'Constance'

Camellia japonica 'Akashigata' or 'Lady Clare' in Eccleston Square

pink flowers, to about 5½in (14cm) across, are produced freely in mid-season and have slightly reflexed petals (occasionally streaked with white) which surround a central boss of stamens and white petaloids. This very popular and well-known variety has been given (under the name of 'Lady Clare', by which it is generally known in Europe and the USA) both an Award of Merit, and Award of Garden Merit by the Royal Horticultural Society. It was introduced from Japan into Europe by the Belgian nursery of Louis van Houtte in the late 19th century.

Camellia japonica 'Guilio Nuccio'

37

Old varieties of *Camellia japonica* in Wuxi, China

Camellia japonica 'Teringa'

Camellia japonica **'Ginyo-tsubaki'**
(syn. 'Ginyô-yasuri') A variety with unusual and attractive leaves which are silvery green with dark green, very serrated edges. The small, single, deep pink flowers with a good central boss of yellow stamens are very simple, making a wonderful contrast with the foliage early in the season. Raised in Izu Oshima, Japan. This plant is not available commercially in Britain at the moment, which is a pity as it deserves to be more widely known; we include it here to try to create some demand.

Camellia japonica **'Katie'** A fast grower with good, dark green leaves and very large flowers, to 6in (15cm) across, early in the spring. Petals deep reddish-pink surrounding a good central boss of stamens. Raised by Nuccio's Nurseries, California, USA, where it first flowered in 1976.

Camellia japonica **'Odoratissima'** (syn. 'La Graciola') An attractive old variety with an upright habit and slightly fragrant flowers (hence

Camellia japonica 'Ginyo-tsubaki' at Nuccio's Nurseries

Camellia japonica 'Mattie Cole'

Camellia japonica 'Katie'

the name). The large, semi-double rose-pink flowers appear from mid- to late spring. Raised by M. Guilfoyle in Australia and listed in his catalogue in 1866.

***Camellia japonica* 'Mattie Cole'**   This has large, single, rather flat, carmine-pink flowers, to about 4½in (12cm) across. Raised by C.F. Cole of Victoria, Australia.

***Camellia japonica* 'Teringa'**   An upright grower, densely clothed with dark green, serrated leaves and large numbers of flowers. The single, reddish-pink (*too pink in our picture*) flowers have 5–7 slightly recurved petals, surrounding a very attractive column of golden-yellow stamens. Raised in Melbourne, Victoria, Australia by Mrs Hume-Turnbull.

C. japonica 'Odoratissima' at Mount Edgcumbe

CAMELLIA JAPONICA

Camellia japonica 'Ruth Kemp'

Camellia japonica 'Alison Leigh Woodroof'
An upright grower, this variety has small, simple, semi-double flowers, pale pink at the centre, becoming a deeper shade of pink towards the outer margins. Raised in 1955 in California, USA.

Camellia japonica 'Furô-an'   An elegant bush of upright habit with very dark green, glossy leaves and medium-sized, pale pink single blooms. The overall effect of the flower is bowl-shaped, with a spreading mass of stamens in the centre. A Japanese seedling of 'Taro-an'.

Camellia japonica 'Hanafûki' (syns. 'Mrs Howard Asper', 'Chalice')   An upright but slow-growing plant with very dark green, serrated leaves and pink, semi-double flowers. A seedling from Japan, whose exact origins are unknown, but which has existed since about the 1880s. 'Hanafûki Variegated' is a form with pink flowers blotched with white.

Camellia japonica 'Spencer's Pink'

'Furô-an'

Camellia japonica 'Alison Leigh Woodroof'

Camellia japonica 'Hanafûki' in Eccleston Square, London

Camellia japonica 'Nuccio's Carousel'
A medium-sized, moderately vigorous, upright bush, with large semi-double flowers with pale pink petals becoming darker at the margins. Raised by Nuccio's Nurseries, California, USA in 1972.

Camellia japonica **'Ruth Kemp'** A rose-pink, medium-sized semi-double camellia with rounded, notched petals and an attractive central whorl of stamens and smaller petals. Raised at Camellia Grove, New South Wales, Australia and available since the 1940s.

Camellia japonica **'Spencer's Pink'** (syn. 'Lady Spencer') A variety with medium-sized single, pale pink flowers, each with a central cluster of golden stamens. This seedling of unknown parentage, originated in Australia at the turn of the century.

Camellia japonica 'Nuccio's Carousel'

Camellia japonica 'Vosper's Rose'   *Camellia japonica* 'Erin Farmer'

Camellia japonica 'Betty Cuthbert'
A medium-sized shrub with a spreading
habit of growth, broad, dark green
leaves and large, informal double
flowers, to 4in (10cm) across. The
20–30 petals are a warm, pale pink
and surround a cluster of stamens
and petaloids. A seedling of
'Yoibijin', selected by
E.G.Waterhouse of New South
Wales, Australia and named after an
Olympic gold medallist.

Camellia japonica 'Erin Farmer'
(syn. 'Aierlan Cunmin')   An upright,
vigorous grower with good, dark green
leaves and attractive flowers, to 4½in
(12cm) across, in spring. These are semi-
double, with pink outer petals, paler pink inner
petals and a mixture of golden stamens and pale
pink petaloids in the centre. Raised in South
Carolina, USA by Mr and Mrs H.E. Ashby.

'Jennifer
Turnbull'

Camellia japonica 'Betty Cuthbert'

Camellia japonica 'Jennifer Turnbull'

A spreading bush with bright green leaves and beautifully simple, single pink flowers to about 4in (10cm) across early in spring. It is a seedling of 'Henry Turnbull' raised by Mrs Hume Turnbull of Victoria, Australia in 1959, using 'Spencer's Pink' as a grandparent.

Camellia japonica 'Peach Blossom' (syn.

'Fleur Dipater') A compact variety which tends to make a spreading bush as it gets older, with dark green, leathery, slightly twisted leaves. The semi-double, medium-sized flowers, to 3½in (9cm) across, consist of up to 20 light pink petals, which are often slightly notched at the end, surrounding a central mass of intermixed stamens and petaloids. This European variety has been grown under several different names and its exact origins are unknown, although it has been commercially available since the early 20th century.

Camellia japonica 'Tomorrow Park Hill'

An upright, vigorous grower, this sport of 'Tomorrow Variegated' was selected by Mrs R. Peer of Hollywood, California, USA in 1960. Its large flowers, to 5in (13cm) across, are sometimes described as semi-double, but we think it is peony-form, with a mass of pale pink petals interspersed with stamens in the centre of the flower.

Camellia japonica 'Vosper's Rose'

A vigorous but compact shrub with medium-sized, semi-double, pale pink flowers and a central boss of stamens interspersed with petaloids. A seedling of 'Spencer's Pink' raised by Mrs J. Vosper of New Zealand in the 1960s.

Camellia japonica 'Tomorrow Park Hill'

Camellia japonica 'Peach Blossom'

Camellia japonica 'Ave Maria' at Mount Edgcumbe

Camellia japonica 'Ave Maria'   A seedling of 'Paeoniaeflora', this has dark green leaves with serrated edges and small, pale pink peony-form flowers, to about 2in (5cm) across in spring. Selected by C. Breschini of California, USA in the 1940s.

Camellia japonica 'Cathy Becher'
An informal double with rose-pink flowers to 4½in (12cm) wide. The leaves are mid-green with serrated edges and pointed tips. Raised in New South Wales, Australia by Mrs D.M. Andrew and first flowered in 1954.

Camellia japonica 'Emily Wilson'
A vigorous, upright grower with glossy, dark green leaves with serrated edges and pointed tips. The shell-pink flowers, to 4½in (12cm) across, are incomplete doubles, with many petals surrounding a central mass of stamens and petaloids. A seedling of unknown parentage which first flowered in 1949, raised by A.T. Wilson of South Carolina, USA. 'Emily Wilson Variegated' (*not shown here*) is a variegated sport with pale pink and white flowers.

Camellia 'Harugasumi'   A hybrid between *C. japonica* 'Snow Bell' and *C. lutchuensis*, with a spreading habit and medium green leaves.

The small, soft pink semi-double flowers, to 2in (5cm) across, usually appear in late winter and early spring. Raised by Longley & Parks, USA in 1947. Note: our specimen has sooty leaves, which usually indicate the presence of aphids or scale insects – for advice on how to rid plants of diseases and disorders see pages 6–7.

'Cathy Becher'

CAMELLIA JAPONICA

Camellia japonica 'Laurie Bray' at Mount Edgcumbe

Camellia japonica 'Laurie Bray' An upright but bushy grower with dark green, slightly curving leaves and plenty of blooms in spring. The flowers are pale pink, semi-double or peony-form, to about 4½in (12cm) across. Raised by G. Linton of New South Wales, Australia, where it first flowered in 1952. 'Laurie Bray Variegated' (*not illustrated here*) is a sport whose flowers are pale pink blotched with white.

'Emily Wilson'

C. japonica 'Harugasumi' at Marwood Hill, Devon

45

CAMELLIA JAPONICA

Camellia japonica 'Annie Wylam'

Camellia japonica 'Annie Wylam'

A medium-sized shrub with an upright habit and dark green leaves, which blooms in mid-spring. The flowers are peony-form or sometimes rose-form double in cooler climates, and are medium-sized, to about 3½in (9cm) across, with wavy rose-pink petals which tend to be a shade darker at the margins. Raised by W. Wylam, California, USA.

Camellia japonica 'Debutante'

Camellia japonica 'Ballet Dancer'

A compact but upright grower with peony-form flowers in spring. The petals are quite pointed at the tip and very pale pink with deeper pink margins. Parentage unknown, but originated in the USA. 'Ballet Dancer Variegated' (*not illustrated here*) is a sport with white blotches on otherwise pink petals.

Camellia japonica 'Incarnata' (syn. 'Lady Hume's Blush' and many others)

A slow growing shrub with a spreading habit, mid-green leaves and pale pink, formal double flowers to 3½in (9cm) across. Its exact origins are unknown, but it was brought from China to Lady Amelia Hume in England in 1806, hence the synonym. A lovely old variety, this was originally listed in 1812 as 'flore pleno incarnato', then as 'The Blush Camellia' in 1816, the current name being finally applied in 1818, when it was illustrated in Loddige's *Botanical Cabinet*, a popular horticultural journal of the time.

Camellia japonica 'Ballet Dancer'

Camellia japonica 'Incarnata' in the Camellia House at Chiswick House

***Camellia japonica* 'Debutante'**
(syn. 'Sarah C. Hastie') A well-known
and deservedly popular variety, this
medium-sized bush bears large numbers
of attractive, pale pink flowers once it is
established. Peony-form flowers, to
about 3in (8cm) across, appear in spring.
Its exact origins seem to be shrouded in
mystery, but it has appeared in
American catalogues (originally
under the name 'Sarah C. Hastie')
since the beginning of the 20th
century. It has given rise to a
number of sports and
seedlings (*not illustrated here*)
including 'Debutante
Blush' and 'Gladys
Marie', and has been
used in hybridizing
to produce plants
such as 'Debbie'
(*see page 92*).

'Debutante'

***Camellia japonica* 'Berenice Perfection'**
A vigorous, upright grower with formal double flowers in mid-spring. The flowers are shell-pink, slightly deeper in colour at the margins, with a very attractive and well-formed centre to the bloom. This is best grown in a greenhouse in Britain and other cooler climates if the flowers are not to be spoilt by bad weather. Raised by Nuccio's Nurseries, California, USA in 1965.

***Camellia japonica* 'Commander Mulroy'**
A medium-sized, upright bush, this is suitable for growing in a large pot or other container if required. The formal double flowers, to about 3in (8cm) across, have white or very pale pink petals, the outer ones being edged with a deeper shade of pink. Raised by T. Patin of Louisiana, USA, parentage unknown.

Camellia japonica 'Desire'

C. japonica 'Nuccio's Jewel' at Nuccio's Nursery

Camellia japonica 'Berenice Perfection'

CAMELLIA JAPONICA

Camellia japonica **'Desire'** A vigorous, upright grower with good dark green foliage and a long flowering season. The flowers are formal double to about 4in (10cm) across, and are pale pink in colour, with the outer petals being a darker shade; the central closed bud is very distinctive. Raised by D. Feathers of California, USA in 1973 using 'Dr Tinsley' and 'Debutante' (*see page 47*) as parents.

Camellia japonica **'Nuccio's Jewel'** A slow grower with flowers that are formal double but peony-form in the centre. The petals are pink, shaded with white in the centre and towards the base. A good bushy plant with flowers from mid- to late spring. Raised by Nuccio's Nurseries, California, USA in 1970.

Camellia japonica 'Commander Mulroy'

Camellias in the national collection at Mount Edgcumbe, Cornwall

CAMELLIA JAPONICA

Camellia japonica 'Ivory Tower'

Camellia japonica 'Alba Plena' An upright, bushy, but slow-growing plant, this is one of the oldest and best double white camellias available. The small, dark matt green, conspicuously veined leaves are slightly twisted. The pure white, formal double flowers, to about 4in (10cm) across, consist of numerous symmetrically overlapped (imbricated) petals. They open in succession in spring; this flowering time can be extended, if the flowers are protected from frost and wind damage by growing under glass in cooler countries. It was brought back to England from China in 1792 by Captain Connor of the East Indiaman *Carnatic*.

Camellia japonica 'Duchessa di Montpensier' A large, creamy white, formal double with beautiful very dark green, glossy leaves. This old variety was raised in Florence, Italy by Gattai in 1851.

Camellia japonica 'Fimbriata' An unusual formal double white camellia with distinctive 'pinked' flowers. This sport of 'Alba Plena' occurred in China and was brought to England in 1816 for Colvil's nursery in the King's Road, Chelsea. We have seen this sport occurring again on a bush of 'Alba Plena' at Caerhays Castle in Cornwall, England.

C. japonica 'Fimbriata' at Caerhays Castle

Camellia japonica 'Matterhorn'

Camellia japonica 'Duchessa di Montpensier'

CAMELLIA JAPONICA

Camellia japonica 'Nuccio's Gem'
An upright shrub with beautiful glossy, dark green leaves which make a wonderful foil for the pure white formal double flowers, to 4in (10cm) across. As it tends to bloom relatively early in the spring it is better grown under glass in cool climates to prevent weather damage to the flowers. Raised from a chance seedling by Nuccio's Nurseries, California, USA in 1952.

Camellia japonica 'Ivory Tower' A medium-sized, compact bush with large, white, formal double flowers in spring. Raised by Shackelford, Georgia, USA.

'Paolina Maggi'

'Nuccio's Gem'

Camellia japonica 'Paolina Maggi'
A beautiful, very formal double with waxy white flowers that have pointed petals and the occasional stripe of raspberry-pink colour. An old variety, this was raised in 1859 by Onofrio Maggi of Brescia, Italy. It has given rise to several sports.

Camellia japonica 'Matterhorn' An upright bush, densely covered with good dark green leaves on pendent branches. The medium-sized, very formal double, rather flat, white flowers usually appear rather late in the spring. Raised by D. Feathers of California, USA.

Camellia japonica 'Alba Plena'; an old bush at Chiswick House

Camellia japonica 'Onetia Holland'

Camellia japonica 'Trewithen White'

Camellia japonica 'Andromeda'   A seedling of the old variety 'Gauntlettii', raised by Prof. E.G.Waterhouse of Gordon, New South Wales, Australia, which flowered first in 1958. Flowers semi-double, white occasionally streaked with pink, with a central column of staminodes.

Camellia japonica 'Madge Miller' (syn. 'Chandleri Alba')   Possibly a seedling of 'Elegans', raised by H. K. Miller of Monticello, Florida and first recorded in 1941. Flowers white, medium-sized to 3in (8cm) across, double, but showing some stamens, of good substance, standing up well to rain.

Camellia japonica 'Onetia Holland'
A seedling of unknown parentage, raised by J.A. Holland of Upland, California and described in 1955. Flowers large, 4½–6½in (12–16cm) across, semi-double, white with mixed stamens and petaloids. Leaves large; growth compact.

Camellia japonica 'Snow Chan'
A sport of 'Shiro Chan', found by Nuccio's Nurseries, Altadena, California in 1957. Flowers anemone-form, white, semi-double, with a central boss of narrow petaloids.

Camellia japonica 'Trewithen White'
A large, peony-form white, probably raised in Cornwall, England in the 1970s.

Camellia japonica 'Le Lys' (syn. 'Madame Victor de Bisschop')   A white semi-double of medium size with a central cluster of golden stamens, sometimes mixed with petaloids. Flowers early in the spring. Raised in Belgium and listed in a catalogue in 1914.

'Le Lys'

Camellia japonica 'Madge Miller' at Marwood Hill, Devon

Camellia japonica 'Andromeda'

Camellia japonica 'Snow Chan'

Camellia japonica 'White Empress' at Mount Edgcumbe, Cornwall

Camellia japonica 'Shiragiku'

Camellia japonica 'Mrs Bertha A. Harms'

Camellia japonica 'Angel'

***Camellia japonica* 'Angel'**   A seedling of unknown parentage, raised by Mrs Elizabeth Councilman of Elmonte, California and described in 1955. Flowers white, medium, 4–4¼in (10–11cm) across, semi-double, with a few petals among the stamens, in mid- to late spring. Leaves ovate; growth pendulous.

***Camellia japonica* 'Gauntlettii'** (syns. 'Lotus', 'Sodegakushi')   An old Japanese variety which originated in the Kanto area of Shigoku and was imported by Gauntlett's Nursery from the Yokahama Nursery Company in 1909. Flowers large, 4¾in (12.5cm) across, cup-shaped, semi-double with a few yellow stamens. Shrub with a tendency to pale green leaves and an open habit.

***Camellia japonica* 'Mrs Bertha A. Harms'**
A cross between 'Lady Clare' and 'Gauntlettii'

CAMELLIA JAPONICA

Camellia japonica 'Gauntlettii' at Mount Edgcumbe, Cornwall

('Sodekakushi'), raised by H.H. Harms of Portland, Oregon, which flowered first in 1947. Flower buds rose-shaped; flowers semi-double, almost white with recurving petals, 4¾–6in (12.5–15cm) across. Blooms mid- to late spring.

Camellia japonica **'Shiragiku'** (syns. numerous and confusing but often called 'Purity') A very ancient variety, this large white formal double has been known under various names since at least 1680.

Camellia japonica **'White Empress'** Raised from seed imported from Japan by K. Sawada of Mobile, Alabama. Flowers large, 4¾–6in (12.5–15cm) across, semi-double with a mass of yellow stamens. Leaves large, narrowly ovate.

Camellia japonica **'White Nun'** A seedling of unknown parentage, raised by McGaskill of Pasadena, California and named in 1959. Flowers large, to 5in (13cm) across, semi-double, white with wide reflexing petals distinct from the central tuft of stamens.

'White Nun'

Camellia japonica 'Kamo-honnami'

Camellia japonica 'Silver Anniversary'

Camellia japonica 'Yukimi-guruma'

Camellia japonica 'Alba Simplex' (also called 'White Swan') A seedling of 'Variegata', raised by William Rollisson & Sons of Tooting, near London in 1813. Flowers single, white with the occasional red fleck, around 3¼in (8.5cm) across, with the stamens joined in their lower third.

Camellia japonica 'Hakutsuru' (syn. 'White Crane') An old Japanese variety, first recorded in 1912. One of the Higo group of *Camellia japonica*, in which the flowers are single, flat, with a large central ring of stamens. Flowering in late spring.

Camellia japonica 'Kamo-honnami'
A Japanese variety, first recorded in 1934, with large, single white flowers, 4–4½in (10–12cm) across, with an upright tuft of stamens.

Camellia japonica 'Sea Foam' A pure white formal double or semi-double, raised in North America and first recorded in 1962. This forms an upright shrub.

Camellia japonica 'Yukimi-guruma' (Snow Viewing Carriage) A traditional Japanese variety,

first recorded in Japan 1859 and imported to America in 1932. A single white, with a wide ring of pale yellow stamens with golden anthers. 'Devonia' and 'Alba Simplex' are very similar.

Camellia japonica 'Silver Anniversary'
Flowers semi-double, white, with petaloids among the stamens; around 5in (13cm) across. Launched by Nuccio's Nursery, Altadena, California in 1960.

'Silver Anniversary'

Camellia japonica 'Sea Foam'   *Camellia japonica* 'Hakutsuru'

Camellia japonica 'Alba Simplex' in Eccleston Square, London

Camellia japonica 'Pompone' at Chiswick House   *Camellia japonica* 'Finlandia'

Camellia japonica 'Melody Lane' in Eccleston Square, London

Camellia japonica 'Finlandia Variegated'
Thought to be an old Japanese variety, imported to Europe and named in America in 1944. Flowers semi-double with wavy petals, white streaked with red.

Camellia japonica 'Finlandia' Probably a sport of 'Finlandia Variegated', which is thought to be an old Japanese variety. This variety was named in 1937 and originated in the old Busch Gardens, California. Flowers white, medium-sized, 4in (10cm) across, semi-double, with a few petals among the stamens, in mid- to late spring.

Camellia japonica 'Lady Vansittart'
(syn. 'Lady Vansittart Lanarth')
An old variety, imported from Japan by Van Houtte of Brussels, Belgium and named in 1887. Flowers semi-double, white with pink streaks and blotches. This is the parent of many sports.

Camellia japonica 'Melody Lane' Raised by E.W. Miller of Escondido, California and named in 1951. Flowers large, semi-double, with some central petaloids, pink striped with red, 4¼–4¾in (11–12.5cm) across.

Camellia japonica 'Pompone' An ancient Chinese variety imported to Kew in 1810. Flowers 3–4in (8–10cm) across, peony-flowered, generally white with pink streaks, but often variable in colour and sometimes white, red and pink on the same bush.

'Finlandia Variegated'

'Melody Lane'

Camellia japonica 'Lady Vansittart'

CAMELLIA JAPONICA

Camellia japonica 'Paul Jones Supreme'

Camellia japonica 'Paul Jones Supreme'
A seedling of 'Paul Jones', raised by Prof. E.G.
Waterhouse of Gordon, New South Wales,
Australia, which flowered first in 1958. Flowers
semi-double, white streaked with pink and red.
Paul Jones is an Australian flower painter whose
superb paintings of camellias are famous.

Camellia japonica 'Tricolor Nova' (syn.
'Tricolor de Mathot') A seedling of 'Tricolor'
recorded in 1846. Flowers imbricated, double,
white or pale pink with crimson streaks and
stripes. Raised by M. Mathot of Ghent, Belgium.

Camellia japonica 'Gengi-guruma'
An old Japanese variety first
mentioned in 1859. Flowers peony-
form, pink streaked with crimson,
produced late in the spring. Old Japanese
paintings show rather heavier red
markings than are seen here.

'Gengi-guruma'

'Lavinia Maggi'

Camellia japonica 'Lavinia Maggi' (syn.
'Countessa Lavinia Maggi') Flowers striking,
double, white, splashed and striped with carmine
red, 3½in (9cm) across. Raised by Lechi in
Brescia, Italy in the middle of the 19th century,
but first recorded in France in 1858.

Camellia japonica 'William Bartlett'
A shrub of compact growth with formal double,
pale pink flowers streaked with crimson, raised by
William Bartlett of Beecroft, New South Wales
and introduced by Hazelwood Bros. of Eppling,
New South Wales, Australia in 1958.

Camellia japonica 'Lavinia Maggi' in Eccleston Square, London

Camellia japonica 'William Bartlett'

Camellia japonica 'Tricolor Nova'

CAMELLIA JAPONICA

Camellia japonica 'Adolphe Audusson Variegated' in Eccleston Square, London

Camellia japonica '**Adolphe Audusson Variegated**' A variegated sport of 'Adolphe Audusson' with dark red, semi-double flowers, occasionally blotched white, to around 4½in (12cm) across. This plant was first recorded in 1941 but was raised in about 1870 and named after M. Adolphe Audusson of Angers. One of the strongest-growing and hardiest varieties, forming a tall open shrub.

Camellia japonica '**Campari**' A large, formal double pink flower streaked with red, named in 1972. A strong-growing shrub, blooming in mid- to late spring, introduced by Armstrong Nurseries, California.

Camellia japonica '**Eleanor Martin Supreme**' A sport of 'Eleanor Martin', found in 1959 by Caesar Breschini in San Jose, California. Flowers semi-double, red flecked with white or sometimes nearly all white, around 4½in (12cm) across. 'Eleanor Martin' was a seedling of 'Donckelaeri' (*see page 64*).

Camellia japonica '**Little Bit**' Introduced by Dr. J.D. Lawson of Antioch, California in 1958. Flowers 2½in (6cm) across, red or red flecked with white, the 5 or so outer petals clearly differentiated from a dense mass of petaloids.

Camellia japonica '**Vittorio Emanuele II**' A peony-form or imbricated double pink flower, striped and spotted with red, raised by Madoni in Brescia, Italy in 1861. Leaves broad with a blunt tip.

'Adolphe Audusson Variegated'

Camellia japonica 'Vittorio Emanuele II' in Descanso Gardens, California

Camellia japonica 'Eleanor Martin Supreme' at Nuccio's Nursery, Altadena, California

Camellia japonica 'Little Bit'

Camellia japonica 'Campari'

Camellia japonica 'Donckelaeri'

Camellia japonica 'Donckelaeri' One of the first Japanese camellias to come to Europe, this was introduced by Franz von Siebold in 1829. It is now correctly known by its original Japanese name 'Masayoshi', the name of the owner of the original tree in Kurume, Fukuoka, an area famed for its azaleas. The flower is large, around 4½in (12cm) across, double, red with variable white stripes, the stamens fused into a tube. Still a popular variety, with long, pointed leaves.

Camellia japonica 'Elegans Variegated' (syn. 'Chandleri Elegans Var.') A white-blotched form of 'Elegans', anemone-flowered to 4¾in (12.5cm) across. 'Elegans' was a seedling of 'Anemoniflora' raised by Alfred Chandler of Vauxhall, near London in 1823. This variegated form was known in the 19th century.

Camellia japonica 'Imbricata' (syn. 'Imbricata Rubra') An ancient Chinese variety introduced to England from China by John Dampier Parks in 1824. Flowers red, formal double, often streaked with white, to 3¾in (9.5cm) across. Leaves with long, decurved points.

Camellia japonica 'Imbricata'

Camellia japonica 'Mercury Variegated' A white blotched variety of 'Mercury', the blotching said to be caused by virus infection. First recorded in *McCaskill Gardens Newest Camellias* 1957. Flowers semi-double, variously blotched with white, around 4in (10cm) across. 'Mercury' was introduced by William Paul & Company around 1900.

Camellia japonica 'Variegata' (syn. 'Old Double Striped') One of the first Chinese varieties to come to England, arriving in 1792 aboard the *Carnatian East Indiaman* for John Salter of India House. Flowers red, heavily blotched with white, double or semi-double, 2¾–4in (7–10cm) across.

Camellia japonica 'Mercury Variegated'

Camellia japonica 'Elegans Variegated'

Camellia japonica 'Variegata'

Camellia japonica 'Elegans Variegated' underplanted with azaleas at Huntington Garden, California

Camellia japonica 'Variegata' at Chiswick House

Camellia japonica 'Claudia Phelps' A sport of 'Duchess of Sutherland', first recorded in the *Fruitland Nursery Catalogue*, Augusta, Georgia in 1949. Flowers semi-double, pink, irregularly shading to white at the edges.

Camellia japonica 'Countess of Orkney' Raised by Mr Nicholson, gardener to the Earl of Orkney and first recorded in 1847. Flower double, rose- to peony-form, the inner petals being somewhat irregular, white to pale pink, striped with pink. A different camellia, a formal double white streaked with pink, is sometimes called 'Countess of Orkney' in the USA.

Camellia japonica 'Yours Truly' A sport of 'Lady Vansittart', first recorded in the *Fruitland Nursery Catalogue*, Augusta, Georgia in 1947–8. A shrub of medium bushy growth. Flowers semi-double, with narrow, pointed, pink petals, becoming paler towards the margin and edged very pale pink or white.

'Can Can'

Camellia japonica 'Can Can'
A sport of 'Lady Loch' found at Camellia Grove Nursery, St Ives, New South Wales in 1956. Flowers peony-form, pale pink with deeper veins and borders, with a narrow dark edge. Shrub strong and upright.

Camellia japonica 'Captain Blood'
A seedling from Jungle Gardens, Avery, Louisiana recorded first in 1948. Flowers peony-form, the outer petals recurved, red veined with purple. A small but very striking flower, sometimes showing stamens. Shrub upright and rather spindly. 'Dona Herzilia de Freitas Magalhaes' is of similar colour, but has a more untidy flower.

'Yours Truly'

C. japonica 'Captain Blood' at Mount Edgcumbe

C. japonica 'Countess of Orkney'

C. japonica 'Claudia Phelps'

Camellia japonica 'Yours Truly' in Eccleston Square, London, with the red 'Apollo' in the background

Camellia japonica 'Margaret Davis'

Camellia japonica 'Jean Clere'

Camellia japonica 'Augusto Leal de Gouveia Pinto' This variety, first recorded in 1904, is thought to have originated in Portugal in the late 19th century as a white-edged sport of 'Grand Sultan', a deep pink formal double close to or possibly the same as 'Mathotiana'. The flowers, about 4¼in (11cm) across, may sometimes have almost blue shading.

Camellia japonica 'Jean Clere' A white-margined sport of 'Aspasia Macarthur' which appeared on an old tree in Taranaki, New Zealand, and was recorded first in 1969. Flowers peony-form, red, with the white band around the edge variable in width, sometimes to ¼in (6mm) wide.

'Augusto Leal de Gouveia Pinto'

Camellia japonica 'Hikarugenji' (syn. 'Herme') An old Japanese variety, first recorded in 1859. Flowers peony-form, pink edged white with deeper crimson veins. Leaves unusually narrow with long point. Blooms in mid- to late spring.

C. *japonica* 'Tom Thumb' at Nuccio's Nursery

C. *japonica* 'Shuchûka' at Nuccio's Nursery

Camellia japonica 'Shuchûka' An old Japanese variety, first recorded in 1789 in the Kanto area of Japan. Shrub bushy and spreading. Flowers open peony-form, white or very pale pink with a red margin to the wavy petals.

Camellia japonica 'Tom Thumb' A sport of unrecorded origin, discovered by A. Kreuger, San Gabriel, California. Shrub of medium, upright growth. Flowers small, formal double, medium pink with a deeper pink edge to the petals.

Camellia japonica 'Margaret Davis'
A beautiful shrub with formal double white flowers about 4in (10cm) wide, with a narrow pinkish-red edge. A sport of 'Aspasia Macarthur' which appeared in Australia in 1961; propagated by A.M. Davis, Cammary, New South Wales.

'Margaret Davis'

Camellia japonica 'Hikarugenji'

Camellia 'Scentuous' at Nuccio's Nursery, Altadena, California

Camellia 'Tiny Princess'

Camellia 'Freedom Bell'

Camellia japonica subsp. *rusticana* × *C. lutchuensis* at the Savill Garden, Windsor Great Park

Camellia japonica 'Otome'

Camellia japonica 'Otome' at Huntington Gardens, California

Camellia japonica* subsp. *rusticana* × *C. lutchuensis This hybrid, as yet unnamed, attempts to combine the double flowers and hardiness of a *Camellia japonica* subsp. *rusticana*, with the scented flowers of *C. lutchuensis*.

***Camellia* 'Freedom Bell'** A fast-growing, upright or rounded shrub with semi-double, slightly trumpet-shaped flowers of a brilliant red, about 3½in (9cm) across. A hybrid of unknown parentage, introduced by Nuccio's Nurseries in 1965.

***Camellia japonica* 'Otome'** (syn. 'Otome-tsubaki', 'Frau Minna Seidel', 'Pink Perfection') One of the varieties of *C. japonica* subsp. *rusticana*, forming a shrub that grows to 15ft (4.5m) with rather erect habit. Flowers in late winter and early spring, pale pink, formal double, about 4¼in

(11cm) wide, with pale pink petals surrounding yellow stamens. An old Japanese garden variety, recorded in the late 18th century.

***Camellia* 'Tiny Princess'** A delicate plant with semi-weeping habit and small, semi-double, pale pink flowers which have a delicate scent. This hybrid between *C. japonica* 'Akebono' and *C. fraterna*, made by K. Sawada in Mobile, Alabama, first flowered in 1956. Free-flowering, but slow-growing. Hardy to 20°F (−6°C), US zones 9–10.

***Camellia* 'Scentuous'** A loose shrub with small leaves, to 2in (5cm) long, and scented, semi-double flowers 2¾in (7cm) across, white with a pink flush on the back of the petals. A hybrid between *C. japonica* 'Tiffany' and *C. lutchuensis*, raised in New Zealand and bloomed first in 1976. Hardy to 20°F (−6°C), US zones 9–10.

CAMELLIA JAPONICA HYBRIDS

'Cornish Spring'

Camellia 'Cornish Snow'

Camellia 'Cornish Spring'   A large shrub that grows to 12ft (3.5m) with small pink flowers to 2in (5cm) wide appearing in early spring. *Camellia* 'Cornish Spring' is a hybrid between *C. cuspidata* and *C. japonica* 'Rosa Simplex', raised by Miss Gillian Carlyon at Tregrehan in Cornwall in 1950. Very free-flowering, with attractive reddish young growth. Hardy to 10°F (−12°C), US zones 8–10.

Camellia 'Cornish Snow'   A small-leaved hybrid forming a loose bush to 15ft (4.5m) tall and wide. Flowers about 1½in (4cm) across appear in early spring. A hybrid between *C. cuspidata* and *C. saluenensis*, raised by J.C. Williams at Caerhays in Cornwall, England in 1930. Its lax growth habit makes it a more natural-looking shrub than most camellias for planting in woodland, and it is ideal against a dark wall, where it will need occasional trimming back and perhaps tying in to wires. Hardy to 10°F (−12°C), US zones 8–10.

Camellia 'Fragrant Pink'   A hybrid between *C. japonica* var. *rusticana* 'Yoshida' and *C. lutchuensis*, raised by Dr William Ackerman at USDA, Glenn Dale, Maryland, which first flowered in 1964. A shrub of spreading growth, with double bright pink scented flowers around 2¼in (5.5cm) across, with around 12 petals. Hardy to 20°F (−6°C), US zones 9–10.

Camellia 'Spring Mist'   This hybrid between *C. japonica* 'Snow Bell' and *C. lutchuensis*, raised by A.E. Longley and C.R. Parks at Los Angeles State and County Arboretum, first flowered in 1965. Plant with open, spreading growth. Flowers blush-pink, semi-double, around 2in (5cm) across, fragrant and freely produced. Hardy to 20°F (−6°C), US zones 9–10.

'Cornish Snow'

Camellia 'Spring Mist' at Trehanes Nursery, Dorset

Camellia 'Fragrant Pink'

Camellia 'Spring Mist'

Camellia reticulata 'Liuye Yinhong' in Berkeley Botanic Garden, near San Francisco

Camellia reticulata

Camellia reticulata is the finest and largest-flowered of all the camellias. The species originates in western China, so the plants are more tender and heat-tolerant than the japonicas. Many cultivars were raised by the Chinese in Yunnan, and the first of these to come to the west was 'Captain Rawes' which arrived in 1820. Though the individual plants are long-lived, *Camellia reticulata* cultivars have always been scarce because they need to be propagated by grafting and will not root from cuttings. Most are hardy to 20°F (–6°C), US zones 9–10.

PLANTING & PRUNING HELP   *Camellia reticulata* thrives in the same conditions as *C. japonica*, but needs more warmth. Many of the varieties are of rather lax growth and need careful pruning after flowering to keep them shapely; they do not respond well to hard pruning.

Camellia reticulata **'Mary Williams'**   This is one of the best of the named seedlings of the wild *Camellia reticulata*, raised at Caerhays Castle, Cornwall from seed collected by Robert Fortune near Tenchung, formerly Tengyueh, in SW Yunnan in 1932. It forms a large shrub with single flowers around 4¾in (12.5cm) across.

Camellia reticulata cultivar   We photographed this striking flower in the Descanso Gardens in La Canada, near Los Angeles, California. Ralf Peer of the Descanso Gardens was one of the first introducers of Kunming *reticulata* camellias to the west from China in 1948.

Camellia reticulata **'Captain Rawes'**   This was the first *Camellia reticulata* to be introduced by Captain Rawes in 1820. He gave the plant to Thomas Carey Palmer of Bromley, Kent, and it

Camellia reticulata cultivar

Camellia reticulata 'Tsueban'

Camellia reticulata 'Captain Rawes'

Camellia reticulata 'Mary Williams'

flowered first in his conservatory in 1826. John Lindley drew up the original description of *Camellia reticulata* from Palmer's plant, and it was soon grown in other conservatories and in gardens in Cornwall. The specimen shown here at Chatsworth was planted in 1850 and old specimens are still found in gardens in Cornwall. A large, loose shrub or small tree to 30ft (10m); bright pinkish-red flowers 5½–6¾in (14–17cm) across, semi-double. The fully-double variety 'Robert Fortune' (syn. 'Pagoda' or 'Pine Cone'), was introduced in early 1850s and named in 1857.

***Camellia reticulata* 'Liuye Yinhong'** (syn. 'Willow Wand', 'Narrow-leaved Shot Silk') This graceful cultivar of *C. reticulata* has rather narrow leaves and light pink flowers with paler stripes, semi-double, up to 6in (15cm) across, produced over a long season into late spring, on a vigorous, tall shrub or small tree. This is one of the best of the traditional Yunnan camellias, introduced to the West in around 1950 from Kunming.

***Camellia reticulata* 'Tsueban'** (or 'Juban', 'Chrysanthemum Petal') A cultivar of *C. reticulata* from Kunming, a formal double pink with flowers to 4in (10cm) across. An early-flowering and vigorous variety, introduced to the Descanso Gardens from China in 1948.

CAMELLIA RETICULATA

Camellia reticulata 'Zhangjiacha'

Camellia 'Arcadia Variegated' A virus-induced variegated form of the hybrid *C. reticulata* 'Mouchang' × *C. sasanqua* 'Bonanza'. It forms a shrub of upright habit with loosely double flowers, salmon-pink blotched with white, 5–6in (13–15cm) across.

Camellia reticulata 'Arch of Triumph' A chance seedling raised by David Feathers in Lafayette, California. It forms a shrub of upright habit with loosely double peony-form flowers, wine-red, up to 6¾in (17cm) across.

Camellia reticulata 'Zhangjiacha' (Butterfly Wing type) A traditional variety from Yunnan cultivated in the Zhangia Temple, Kunming. Flowers loosely semi-double with narrow petals, mauve pink, around 4¼–6in (11–15cm) across.

Camellia reticulata 'Mudancha' or **'Moutancha'** Peony Camellia A traditional variety from Yunnan with large, silvery pink flowers and petals among the conspicuous stamens, around 4¼–6½in (11–16cm) across. It forms a shrub of rather short and rounded habit.

Camellia reticulata 'Nuccio's Ruby' An American variety raised by Nuccio's Nursery at Altadena, California in 1974. Flowers semi-double, around 4¾in (12.5cm) wide with wavy, deep red petals and conspicuous yellow stamens. It forms a shrub of rather upright habit.

Camellia reticulata 'Wanduocha' A semi-double traditional variety from Yunnan, seen here in the courtyard of the Yufeng lamasery near Lijiang, Yunnan. This ancient tree is known locally as the ten-thousand-flower camellia and is reputed to be 500 years old. Flowers 4–6in (10–15cm) across.

Camellia reticulata 'Mudancha'

Camellia 'Arcadia Variegated'

Camellia reticulata 'Zhangjiacha'

Camellia reticulata 'Wanduocha' at the Yufeng lamasery in the foothills of the Lijiang mountains

Camellia reticulata 'Arch of Triumph'

Camellia reticulata 'Nuccio's Ruby'

Camellia reticulata 'Lila Naff'

Camellia reticulata 'Dayinhong'

Camellia reticulata 'Dayinhong' 'Great Shot Silk' A traditional variety from Yunnan, with large pink peony-form flowers and numerous wavy petals among the few stamens, around 4–5in (10–13cm) across. Particularly free-flowering. Said to be a seedling of 'Liuye Yinhong' (*see page 75*).

Camellia 'Francie L.' A hybrid between *C. saluenensis* 'Apple Blosson' and *C. reticulata* 'Buddha', raised by Ed Marshall in the Huntington Gardens, San Marino, California and first flowered in 1960. Flowers reddish with numerous petals around a dense, conspicuous mass of stamens, around 5in (13cm) across.

Camellia 'Interval' A hybrid between *C. reticulata* and *C. japonica*, raised by David Feathers in Lafayette, California and named in 1970. A plant with compact, bushy growth in the open; flowers silvery pink with darker veins, semi-double, to 6¾in (17cm) across when open.

Camellia reticulata 'Lila Naff'
A seedling of 'Houye Diechi', raised by Mrs Ferol Zerkowsky in Slidell, Louisiana, which first flowered in 1958. A sparsely branching bush with semi-double, pale pink petals around a cone of stamens. Flowers cup-shaped, 4–4¾in (10–12.5cm) across.

Camellia 'Royalty' A hybrid between *C. reticulata* 'Chang's Temple' and *C. japonica*,

'Clarise Carlton' raised by T.E. Croson in Simi, California and named in 1970. Plant with medium upright growth. Flowers around 5in (13cm) across, semi-double with ruffled petals around a cone of stamens.

Camellia reticulata 'Trophy' This hybrid of *C. reticulata* makes a strong-growing shrub with double pink flowers of rose form, around 5in (13cm) across, late in the spring.

'Francie L.'

Camellia 'Royalty'

Camellia 'Interval'

Camellia reticulata 'Trophy'

Camellia 'Francie L.'

Camellia 'Maud Messel'

Camellia 'Salutation'

Camellia reticulata hybrids

The hybrids of *Camellia reticulata* shown here need much the same conditions as the cultivars of the species itself, although they may be a little hardier. Most will survive 20°F (–6°C), US zones 9–10, though the hybrids with *C. japonica* may survive 10°F (–12°C), US zone 8.

PLANTING & PRUNING HELP *Camellia reticulata* hybrids thrive in the same conditions as *C. japonica*, but may need more warmth. Because many are of rather lax growth they need careful pruning after flowering to prevent the bushes becoming lank and leggy; they do not respond well to hard pruning. Varieties with large flowers are best grown under glass in areas where spring can be wet and cold.

***Camellia* 'Felice Harris'** (probably *C. sasanqua* 'Narumigata' × *C. reticulata*)   A hybrid raised in 1960 by Howard Asper, California. Flowers like a *C. × williamsii* semi-double with a few small petaloids among stamens, 4¼in (11cm) across.

***Camellia* 'Innovation'**   A seedling of 'William's Lavender' (*C. × williamsii*) crossed with *C. reticulata* 'Crimson Robe', raised by David Feathers in Lafayette, California and named in 1958. Flowers semi-double to peony-form, 4¾in (12.5cm) across, reddish with lavender shading throughout the spring.

'Inspiration'

CAMELLIA RETICULATA HYBRIDS

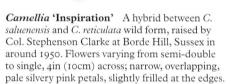

'Felice Harris'

Camellia 'Salutation'

Camellia 'Inspiration' A hybrid between *C. saluenensis* and *C. reticulata* wild form, raised by Col. Stephenson Clarke at Borde Hill, Sussex in around 1950. Flowers varying from semi-double to single, 4in (10cm) across; narrow, overlapping, pale silvery pink petals, slightly frilled at the edges.

Camellia 'Maud Messel' A hybrid between *C.* × *williamsii* 'Mary Christian' and *C. reticulata* 'Hikarugenji' raised by L.C.R. Messel at Nymans, Sussex and named in 1969. Flowers rose form, double, with narrow, overlapping petals around yellow stamens, about 2¾in (7cm) across. Petals pale pink with darker veins.

Camellia 'Salutation' A hybrid between *C. saluenensis* and *C. reticulata* 'Captain Rawes', raised by Col. Stephenson Clarke at Borde Hill, Sussex around 1930. Flowers pale silvery pink, semi-double to single with narrow, overlapping petals, around 4in (10cm) across.

Camellia 'Valleé Knudson' A hybrid between *C. saluenensis* and *C. reticulata* 'Buddha', raised by Howard Asper at Escondido, California in around 1958. Flowers semi-double, around 4½in (12cm) across, cup-shaped with numerous overlapping petals. An excellent shrub of vigorous, compact and upright growth.

Camellia 'Valleé Knudson'

Camellia 'Innovation'

Camellia 'Arbutus Gum'

Camellia 'California Sunset'

Camellia 'Howard Asper'

Camellia 'Harold L. Paige'

Camellia 'Arbutus Gum'   A hybrid between *Camellia reticulata* and *C. japonica*, raised by Frank Maitland, California; a chance seedling which flowered first in 1964. A fast-growing, upright shrub with large, pale or deep pink flowers, semi-double with ruffled petals, around 5in (13cm) across, in mid- to late spring.

Camellia 'California Sunset'   A hybrid between *Camellia sasanqua* × *C. reticulata*, raised by Nuccio's Nurseries, Altadena, California, which first flowered in 1981. A fast-growing, upright shrub, the flowers bright pink, semi-double, with narrow petals, produced early in the spring.

Camellia 'Harold L. Paige'   A hybrid between *C. japonica* 'Adolphe Audusson' and *C. reticulata* 'Crimson Robe', raised by J. Osegueda, Oakland, California, which first flowered in 1969. A vigorous shrub with spreading growth; flowers double, bright red, 5¼in (13.5cm) across, late in the spring.

CAMELLIA RETICULATA HYBRIDS

Camellia 'Otto Hopfer' at Huntington Botanical Gardens, California

Camellia **'Howard Asper'** A hybrid between *Camellia reticulata* 'Damanao' and *C. japonica* 'Coronation' raised by Howard Asper, San Marino, California, which flowered first in 1962. A fast-growing shrub with very large flowers, semi-double with wavy petals, up to 7in (18cm) across.

Camellia **'Lasca Beauty'** A hybrid between *C. reticulata* 'Damanao' and *C. japonica* 'Mrs D.W. Davis', raised by Dr Clifford Parks at the Los Angeles State and County Arboretum, California and grown by David Feathers, which flowered first in 1970. A loose, open shrub with very large flowers, semi-double with thick petals.

Camellia **'Otto Hopfer'** A hybrid between *C. reticulata* 'Crimson Robe' and *C. japonica* 'Lotus' raised by D. Hopfer in San Francisco in 1972. A shrub of upright growth; flowers semi-double, red, very large, around 4¾in (12.5cm) across, in mid-spring.

'Lasca Beauty'

83

Camellia × williamsii 'Donation' at Mount Edgcumbe, Cornwall

Camellia × williamsii

The cultivars of *Camellia × williamsii* are the most free-flowering and easily grown of all camellias, especially in cooler climates. 'Donation', the most popular of the group, always covers itself with the silvery pink flowers which are the commonest colour, derived from the *saluenensis* parent (*see page 12*). Most will survive 10°F (−12°C), US zones 8–10, though the duration of the cold has great effect on the rate of survival. The flowers of *Camellia × williamsii* drop as they die, ensuring a tidy plant, not disfigured by the brown remains of dead flowers.

This group of hybrid camellias was first produced in the early 1930s by J.C. Williams of Caerhays Castle, Cornwall, England by crossing *Camellia japonica* with *Camellia saluenensis*, then a new species, which was raised at Caerhays from seed collected by George Forrest along the Salween river in Yunnan in 1924. Old varieties from Caerhays tend to have single flowers, more modern ones from other raisers have semi-double or double flowers. The leaves are slightly paler and less shiny than those of *C. japonica*, though not as dull as those of *C. saluenensis*. Hairs on the ovary are usually a sign of *C. saluenensis* parentage.

During a visit to the area of the old trials of *C. × williamsii* cultivars at Wisley on a warm day in February, we noticed a delicate but sweet scent which we traced to flowers of *C. × williamsii* 'Mary Jobson'. This scent was also noted by Neil Treseder in *Growing Camellias* (1975), the plant of 'Mary Jobson' being in this case the original at

Caerhays. The same scent is also found in old single-flowered *C. japonica* in Cornish gardens.

PLANTING & PRUNING HELP   *Camellia × williamsii* hybrids thrive in the same conditions as *Camellia japonica*, but are tolerant of cooler conditions. Young plants should be set out with much leaf-mould or ericaceous compost incorporated into the surrounding soil. A mulch of leaf-mould is also a great help in preserving moisture during summer and promoting good growth, as many of the camellia roots are near the surface.

'Donation'

***Camellia* × *williamsii* 'Caerhays'**   A delicate pink semi-double or single-flowered variety, raised at Caerhays in 1948. A hybrid between *Camellia saluenensis* and *C. japonica* 'Lady Clare', retaining something of the spreading and pendulous habit of the latter parent. Flowers around 4in (10cm) across.

***Camellia* × *williamsii* 'Coppelia Alba'**
A single white flower of medium size on a shrub of upright habit, raised by Francis Hanger in around 1955. Hanger was gardener to Lionel de Rothschild at Exbury from 1927, before becoming Curator of the RHS garden at Wisley in 1946–61.

***Camellia* × *williamsii* 'Donation'**   A hybrid between *C. saluenensis* and *C. japonica* 'Donckelarii', raised by Walter Fleming, gardener to Col. Stephenson Clarke at Borde Hill, Sussex in around 1927. Still one of the most popular and spectacular of the hybrids, it produces masses of semi-double, silvery flowers about 4¼in (11cm) across, over a very long season on a rather upright shrub. This variety is probably the most free-flowering of all cultivated camellias.

***Camellia* × *williamsii* 'J. C. Williams'**   Raised by J.C. Williams at Caerhays, Cornwall and named in 1940. An evergreen shrub reaching 15ft (4.5m). The pale pink, single flowers, about 4in (10cm) across, are produced in great abundance. An exceptionally hardy and long-flowering variety.

***Camellia* × *williamsii* 'St Ewe'**   A single-flowered variety with deep pink, cup-shaped flowers, freely produced for a long period on a rather upright shrub. Raised by J.C. Williams at Caerhays, Cornwall and named in 1947.

Camellia × *williamsii* 'Coppelia Alba'

Camellia × *williamsii* 'St Ewe'

C. × *williamsii* 'Caerhays' at Caerhays Castle

Camellia × *williamsii* 'J.C. Williams'

'Francis Hanger'

Camellia × williamsii 'Beatrice Michael'
Raised by J.C. Williams at Caerhays, Cornwall and named in 1954. Similar to 'J.C. Williams' but with deeper pink, single or semi-double flowers around 2¾in (7cm) across and narrower leaves.

Camellia × williamsii 'Elizabeth de Rothschild'   A hybrid between *C. japonica* 'Adolphe Audusson' and *C. saluenensis,* raised by Francis Hanger while gardener to Lionel de Rothschild at Exbury and named in 1951. Flowers semi-double, rose-pink, in mid- to late spring.

Camellia × williamsii 'Elizabeth de Rothschild'

Camellia × williamsii 'Beatrice Michael' at Mount Edgcumbe, Cornwall

Camellia × williamsii 'The Duchess of Cornwall'

Camellia × williamsii 'Margaret Waterhouse'

Camellia × williamsii **'Francis Hanger'**
A single-flowered white variety raised by Francis Hanger at Wisley and named in 1963. Flowers around 3in (8cm) wide, very freely produced. One of the few white *Camellia × williamsii* cultivars, a cross between *C. japonica* 'Alba Simplex' and *C. saluenensis*.

Camellia × williamsii **'Margaret Waterhouse'**
Raised by Prof. E.G. Waterhouse of Gordon, New South Wales, Australia and named in 1955. Flowers semi-double, 3–3½in (8–9cm) across on a vigourous, erect bush.

Camellia × williamsii **'Mary Jobson'**
A sweetly scented variety raised by J.C. Williams at Caerhays, Cornwall and named in 1947. Flowers deep pink, single; leaves shiny for *C. × williamsii*. Bush wide-spreading when mature.

Camellia × williamsii **'The Duchess of Cornwall'**
A hybrid between *C. japonica* 'Adolphe Audusson' and *C. saluenensis*, raised by Miss G. Carlyon at Tregrehan, Cornwall and named in 1980. Flowers double with some stamens, pale silvery pink, 4in (10cm) across on a spreading shrub.

'Mary Jobson'

Camellia × *williamsii* 'Golden Spangles'

'Mildred Goatcher'

Camellia **'Rosemary Sawle'**   A seedling of *C.* 'Barbara Hillier' raised by Miss G. Carlyon at Tregrehan, Cornwall and named in 1973. 'Barbara Hillier' is of doubtful parentage, probably a seedling of the wild form of *C. reticulata*. Flowers of good substance, single, rich pink on a densely bushy shrub.

Camellia × *williamsii* **'Bow Bells'**   A compact bushy shrub, often flowering exceptionally early, bearing large numbers of medium-sized, trumpet-shaped, semi-double pink flowers from mid-winter to late spring. Shrub spreading, becoming pendulous. Particularly recommended for planting against a coo,l north-facing wall. Raised by W.J. Marchant of Wimborne, Dorset and named in 1954. Flowers said to be scented.

Camellia × *williamsii* **'C.F. Coates'**   A hybrid between *C. saluenensis* and *C. japonica* 'Quercifolia' raised at Kew in 1935. Flowers small, single, pink, cup-shaped. Leaves variably forked at the tips, dark, shiny green on a spreading bush.

Camellia × *williamsii* **'Golden Spangles'**
A form of *Camellia* × *williamsii*, very close to 'Mary Christian', with golden variegated leaves, which appeared at Wisley in 1946. Flowers single, rich pink, in early to mid-spring. It is not clear whether this was a mutation of 'Mary Christian' or a separate seedling.

Camellia × *williamsii* 'Golden Spangles'

Camellia × williamsii 'Mildred Goatcher'
A chance seedling, probably from *C.* 'Donation',
raised by Herbert Goatcher at Washington, Sussex
and named in 1977. Similar in size to 'Donation'
but flowers with wider petals of a brighter, deeper
pink.

Camellia × williamsii 'William Carlyon'
A hybrid between *C. japonica* 'Juno' and *C. ×
williamsii* 'Donation', raised by Miss G. Carlyon at
Tregrehan, Cornwall and named in 1973. Flowers
single, reddish-pink, on a spreading bushy shrub.

Camellia × williamsii 'C.F. Coates'

Camellia × williamsii 'William Carlyon' *Camellia × williamsii* 'Bow Bells'

Camellia 'Rosemary Sawle' at Mount Edgcumbe

Camellia × williamsii 'Shocking Pink'

Camellia × williamsii 'Waterlily'

Camellia × williamsii 'Joan Trehane'

Camellia × williamsii 'Bowen Bryant'

Camellia × williamsii **'Bowen Bryant'**

A seedling of *C. saluenensis*, raised by Prof. E. G. Waterhouse in Bowen, New South Wales, and named in 1957. A large, semi-double, rich pink flower with silvery shading, occasionally with an odd petaloid among the stamens. Leaves dark, shiny green, with long narrow points.

Camellia × williamsii **'E. G. Waterhouse'**

A self-sown seedling from the garden of Prof. E.G. Waterhouse in Bowen, New South Wales, Australia. A compact upright shrub, producing formal double, light silvery pink flowers in mid- to late spring.

Camellia × williamsii **'Joan Trehane'**

A hybrid between *C. saluenensis* and *C. japonica* 'Hikarugenji' raised by Les Jury in New Plymouth, New Zealand and introduced by J. Trehane & Son in 1980. Flowers formal double, pink, 4–4½in (10–12cm) across.

Camellia × williamsii **'Shocking Pink'**

A self-sown seedling of *C. saluenensis* from the garden of Prof. E.G. Waterhouse in Bowen, New South Wales, Australia. An upright shrub, producing rose form to formal double rose pink flowers in mid- to late spring.

Camellia × williamsii **'Waterlily'**

A hybrid between *C. saluenensis* and *C. japonica* 'K. Sawada' raised by Felix Jury in Wairara, New Zealand and named in 1967. An upright shrub, producing formal double, rose-pink flowers 4¼in (11cm) across in mid- to late spring.

'E.G. Waterhouse'

Camellia × williamsii 'Anticipation'

'Debbie'

Camellia × williamsii 'Anticipation'

Camellia × williamsii 'Ballet Queen'

Camellia × williamsii 'Anticipation'
A hybrid between *Camellia saluenensis* and
Camellia japonica 'Levathian' raised by Les Jury in
New Plymouth, New Zealand and named in 1962.
Flowers large, peony-form, purplish pink, about
4in (10cm) across, in mid-spring.

Camellia × williamsii 'Ballet Queen'
A hybrid between *C. saluenensis* and *C. japonica*
'Leviathan', raised by Les Jury in New Plymouth,
New Zealand and named in 1976. Flowers peony-
form, silvery salmon-pink, about 4in (10cm)
acros, in mid- to late spring.

Camellia × williamsii 'Debbie' A hybrid
between *Camellia saluenensis* and *C. japonica*
'Debutante', raised by Les Jury in New Plymouth,
New Zealand and named in 1965. Flowers peony-
form, bright pink, about 4in (10cm) across,

Camellia × *williamsii* 'Jury's Yellow' at Trewithen, Cornwall

produced from mid-winter well into spring and dropping cleanly when faded. This is often one of the most striking camellias in any collection.

Camellia × *williamsii* 'Jury's Yellow'

A hybrid between *C.* × *williamsii* (*C. saluenensis* × *C. japonica* 'Daikagura') and *C. japonica* 'Gwenneth Morey', raised by Les Jury in New Plymouth, New Zealand and named in 1976. Flowers anemone-form, about 3in (8cm) across, white, with smaller yellow central petals. Shrub robust and upright when young.

Camellia × *williamsii* 'Rose Bouquet'

A hybrid between *C. saluenensis* and *C. japonica* 'Tiffany' raised by Felix Jury in Wairara, New Zealand and named in 1979. An upright shrub, producing formal double to rose-form, silvery pink flowers 4¾in (12.5cm) across, in mid-spring.

Camellia × *williamsii* 'Rose Bouquet'

Index

INDEX